CHRISTMAS SENTIMENTS

19 NOSTALGIC SONGS ARRANGED BY PHILLIP KEVEREN

— PIANO LEVEL —
EARLY INTERMEDIATE

ISBN 978-1-70516-848-6

Visit Hal Leonard Online at
www.halleonard.com

Visit Phillip at
www.phillipkeveren.com

World headquarters, contact:
Hal Leonard
7777 West Bluemound Road
Milwaukee, WI 53213
Email: info@halleonard.com

In Europe, contact:
Hal Leonard Europe Limited
42 Wigmore Street
Marylebone, London, W1U 2RY
Email: info@halleonardeurope.com

In Australia, contact:
Hal Leonard Australia Pty. Ltd.
4 Lentara Court
Cheltenham, Victoria, 3192 Australia
Email: info@halleonard.com.au

PREFACE

Christmas assignments seemingly never end for arrangers. That is completely fine by me! I never tire of Yuletide tunes – whether classical, traditional carol, jazz, or pop.

This collection focuses primarily on songs from the popular music world. Many of these titles originally appeared in films ("Believe"), others provided hits for popular singers ("Merry Christmas, Darling"). Some of them show up in countless recordings every year ("White Christmas"), while others are more rarely found in the holiday genre ("River").

As you count your blessings this holiday season, I hope these piano arrangements will help you get in the Christmas spirit!

Sincerely,

Phillip Keveren

BIOGRAPHY

Phillip Keveren, a multi-talented keyboard artist and composer, writes original works in a variety of genres from piano solo to symphonic orchestra. He gives frequent concerts and workshops for teachers and their students in the United States, Canada, Europe, and Asia. Mr. Keveren holds a B.M. in composition from California State University Northridge and a M.M. in composition from the University of Southern California.

CONTENTS

ALL IS WELL

Words and Music by MICHAEL W. SMITH
and WAYNE KIRKPATRICK
Arranged by Phillip Keveren

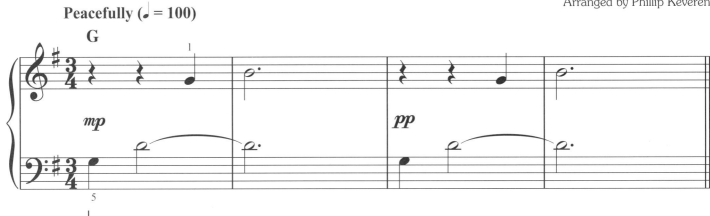

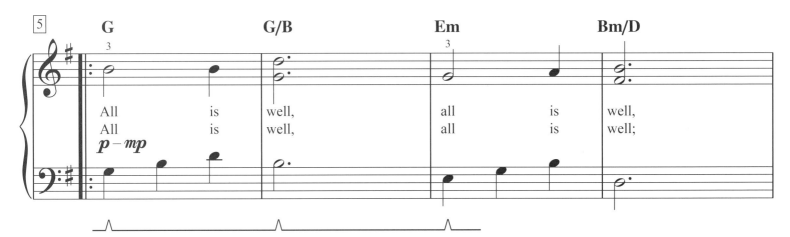

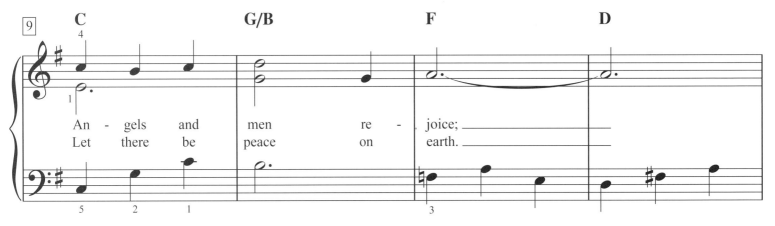

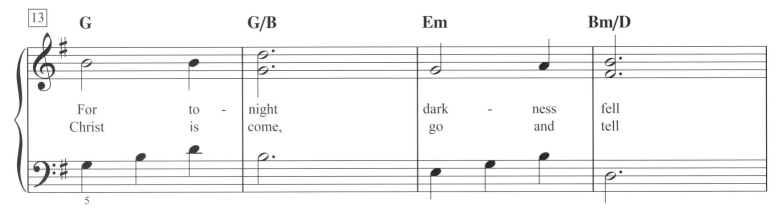

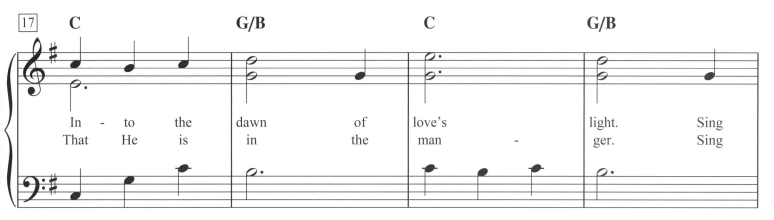

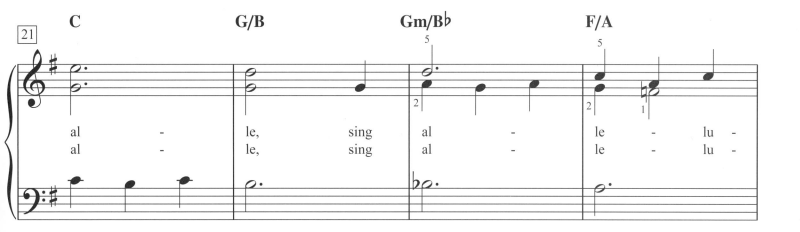

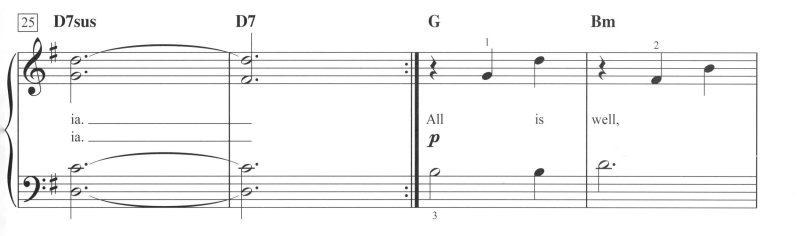

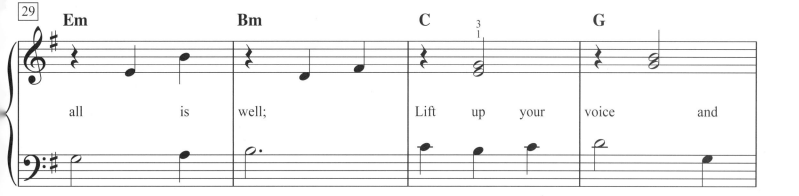

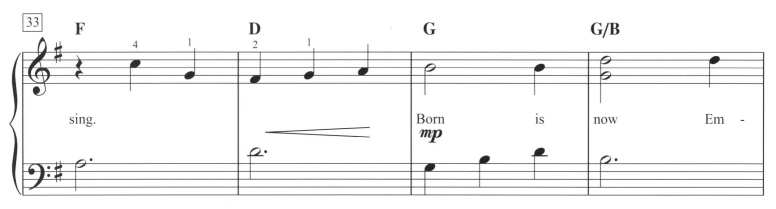

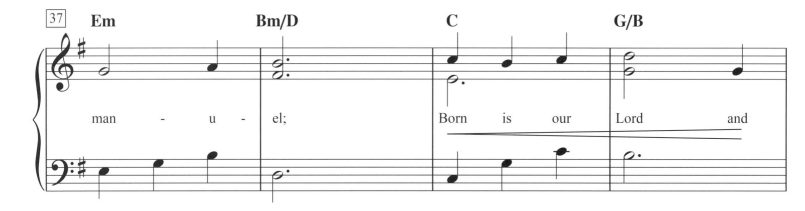

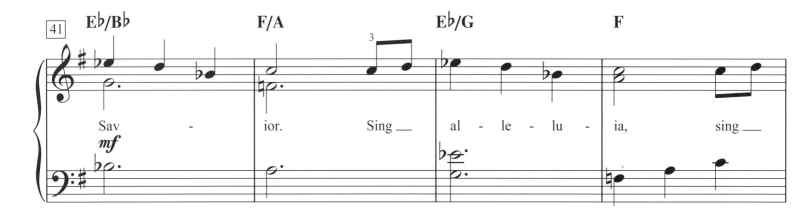

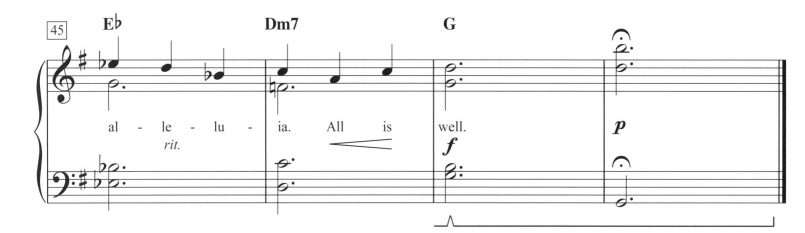

BECAUSE IT'S CHRISTMAS
(For All the Children)

Music by BARRY MANILOW
Lyric by BRUCE SUSSMAN and JACK FELDMAN
Arranged by Phillip Keveren

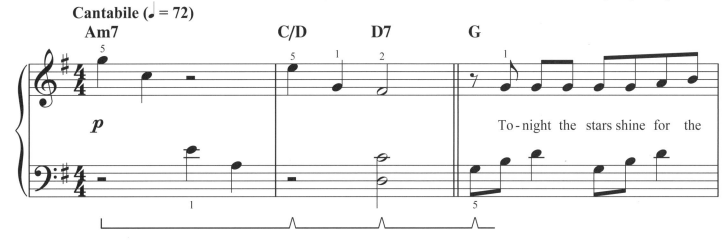

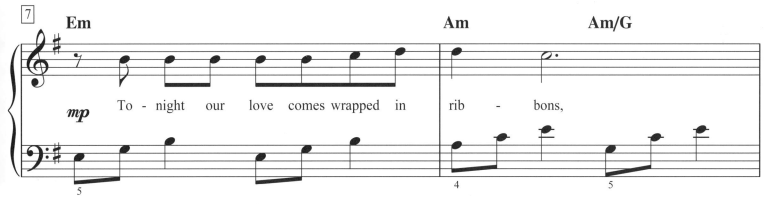

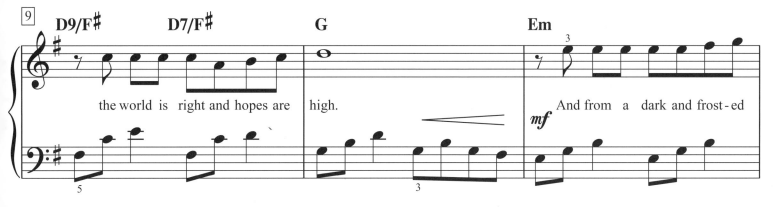

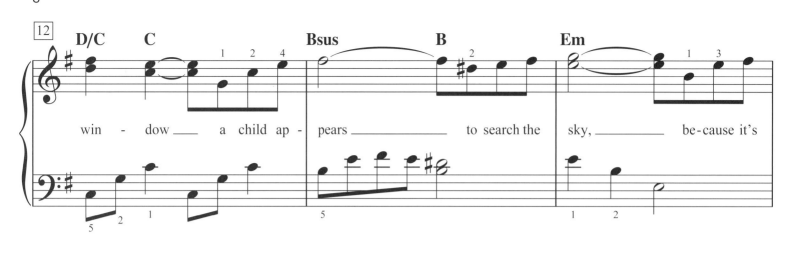

win - dow ___ a child ap - pears _____ to search the sky, _____ be-cause it's

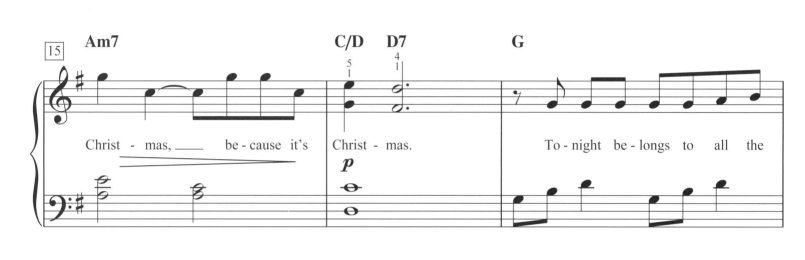

Christ - mas, ___ be-cause it's Christ - mas. To - night be - longs to all the

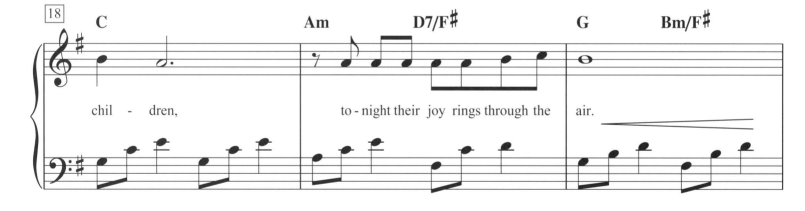

chil - dren, to - night their joy rings through the air.

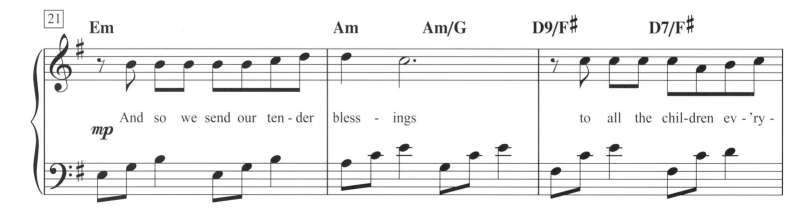

And so we send our ten - der bless - ings to all the chil-dren ev - 'ry -

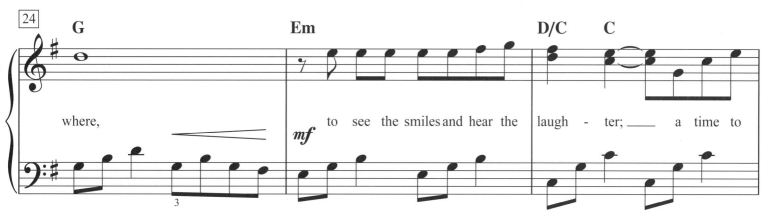

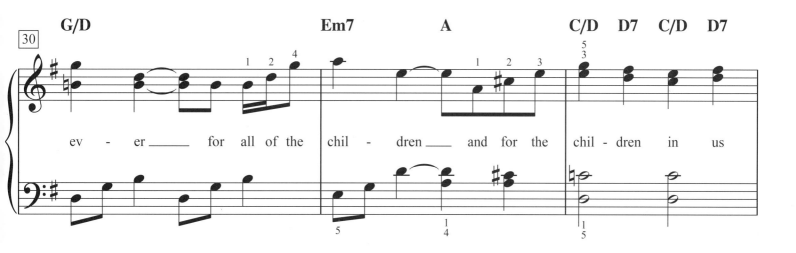

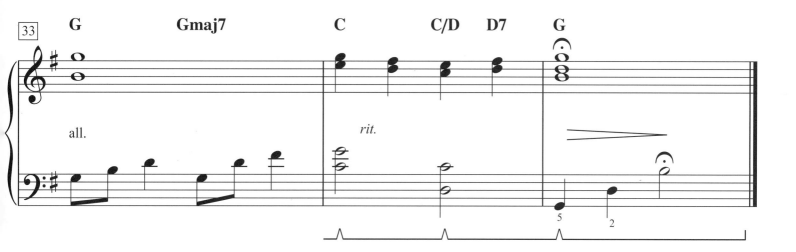

BELIEVE

from Warner Bros. Pictures' THE POLAR EXPRESS

Words and Music by GLEN BALLARD
and ALAN SILVESTRI
Arranged by Phillip Keveren

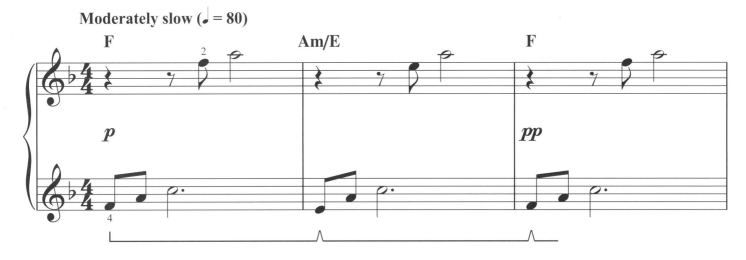

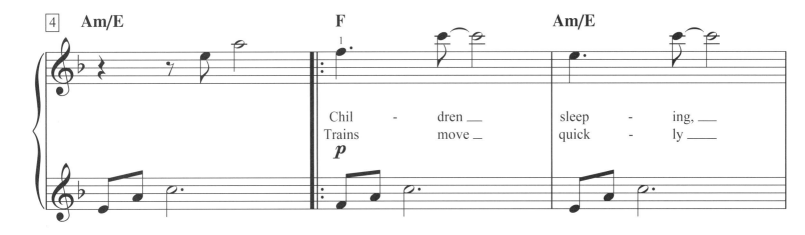

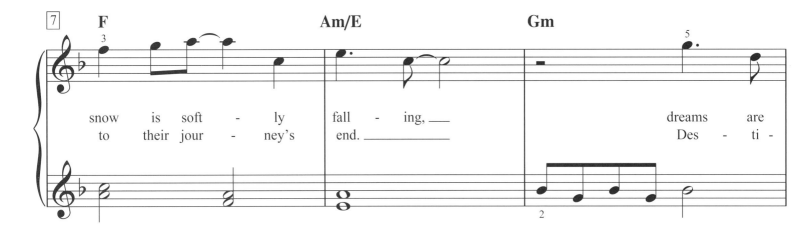

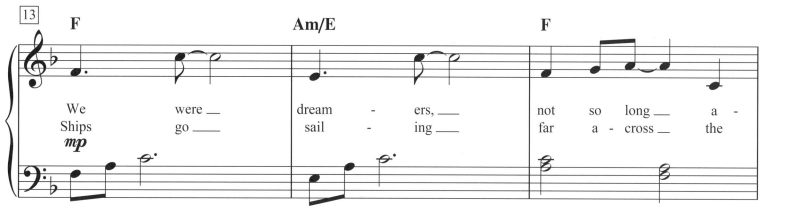

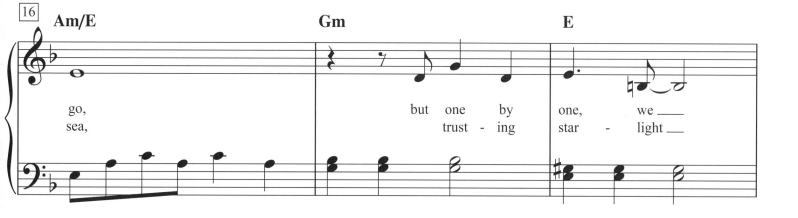

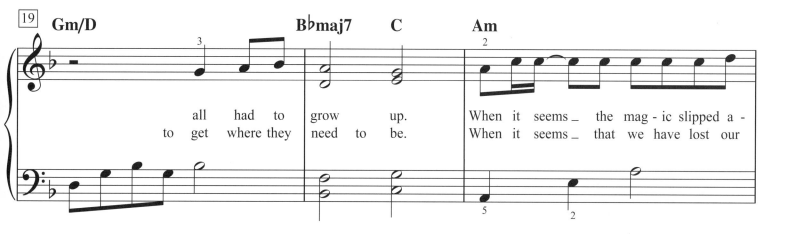

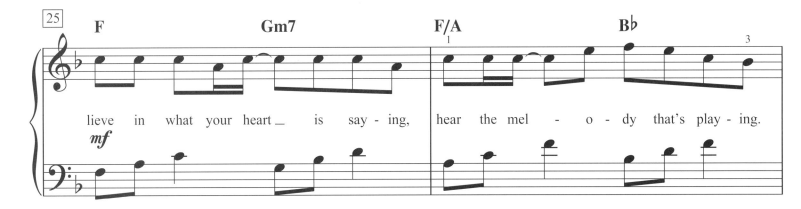

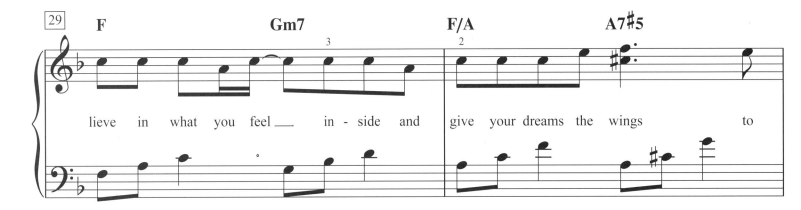

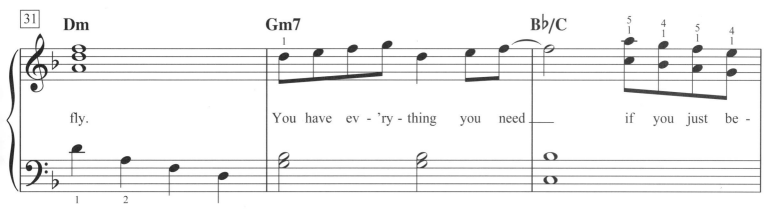

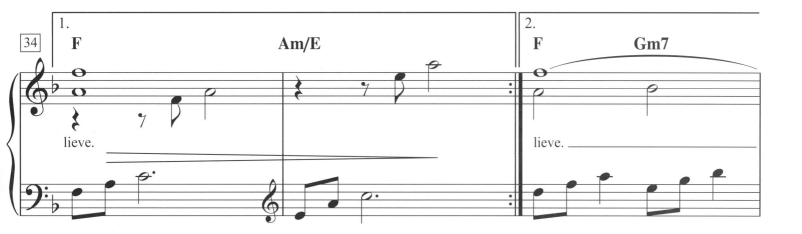

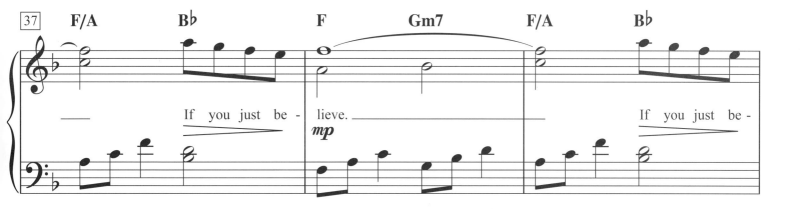

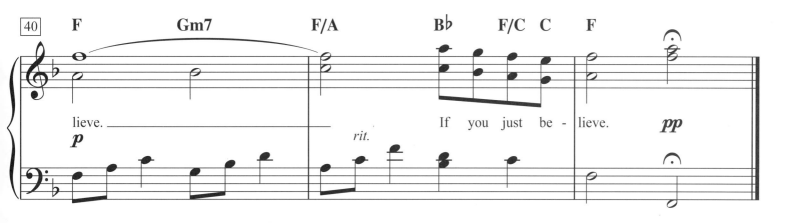

BLUE CHRISTMAS

Words and Music by BILLY HAYES
and JAY JOHNSON
Arranged by Phillip Keveren

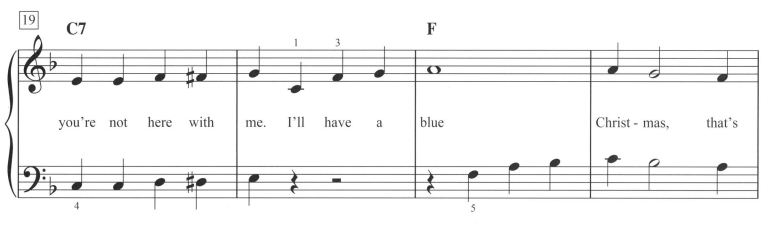

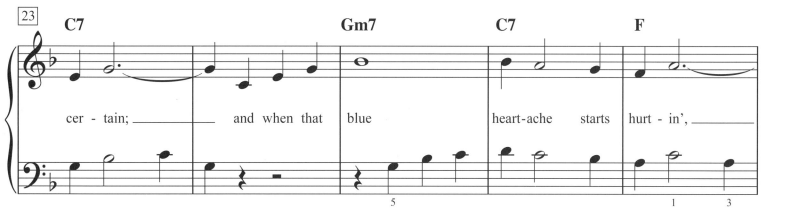

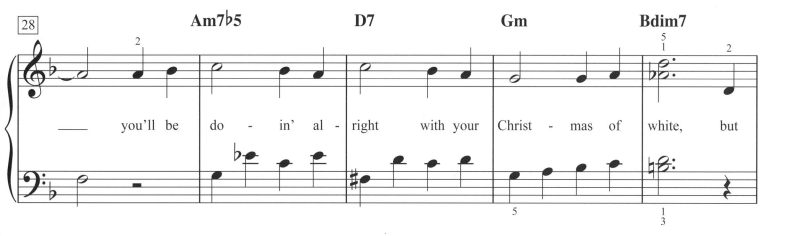

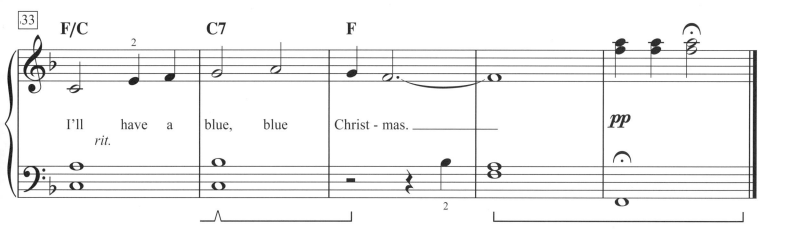

BREATH OF HEAVEN
(Mary's Song)

Words and Music by AMY GRANT
and CHRIS EATON
Arranged by Phillip Keveren

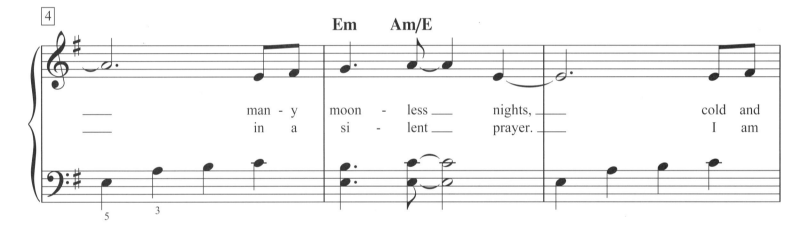

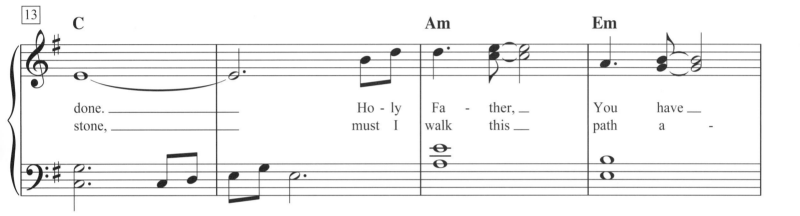

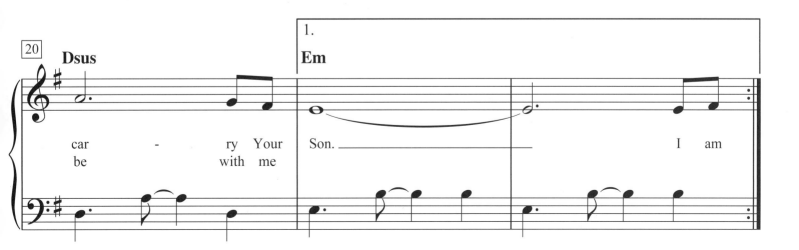

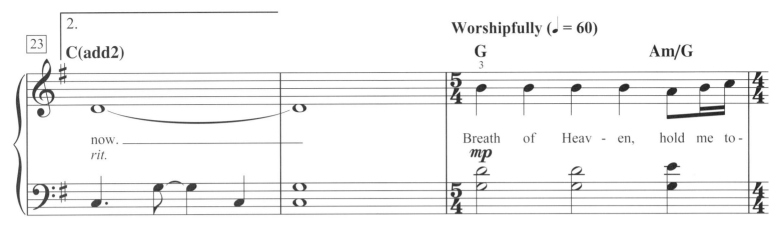

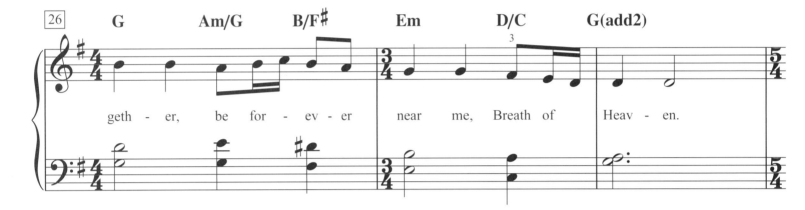

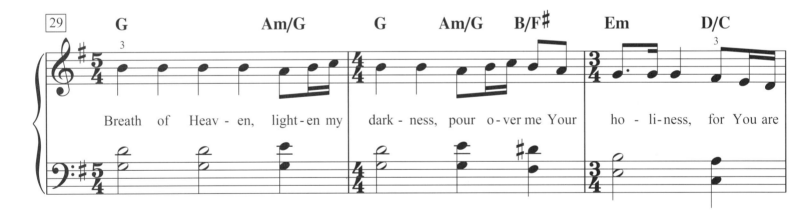

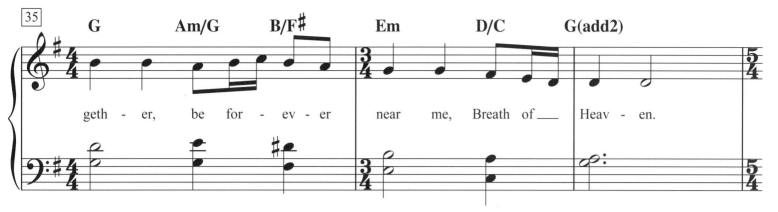

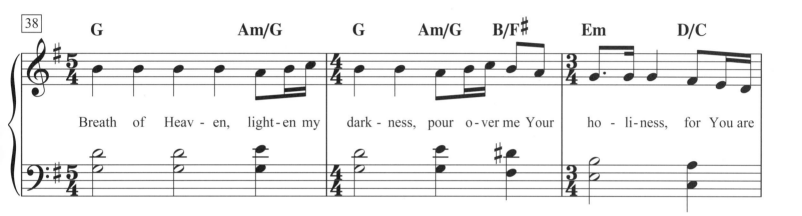

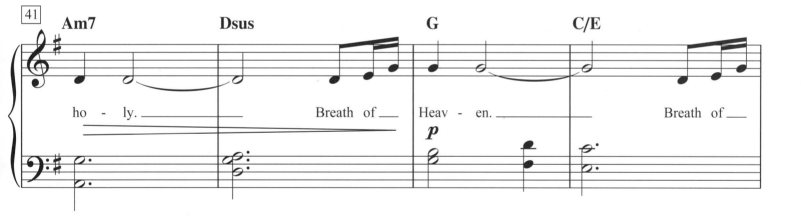

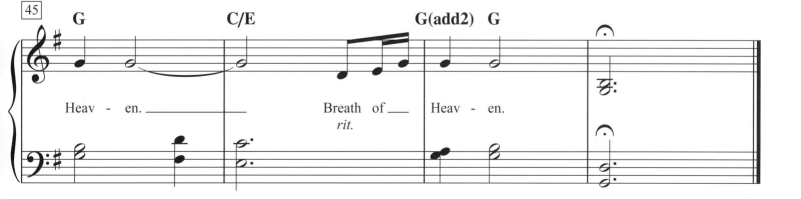

A CHILD IS BORN

Music by THAD JONES
Lyrics by ALEC WILDER
Arranged by Phillip Keveren

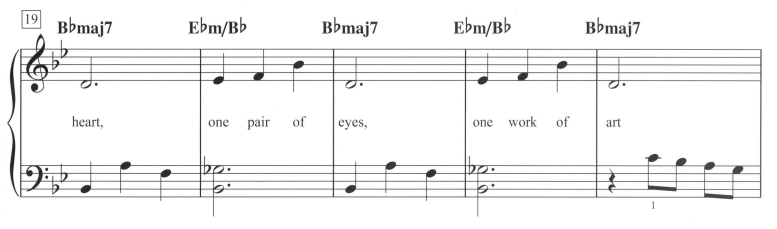

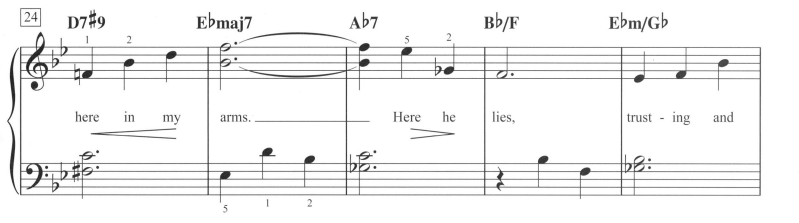

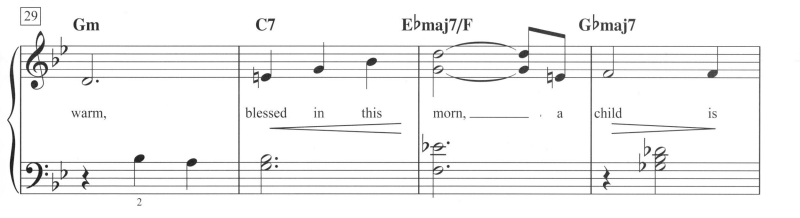

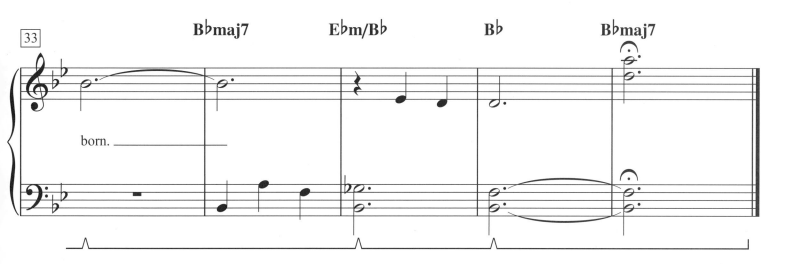

CHRISTMAS TIME IS HERE
from A CHARLIE BROWN CHRISTMAS

Words by LEE MENDELSON
Music by VINCE GUARALDI
Arranged by Phillip Keveren

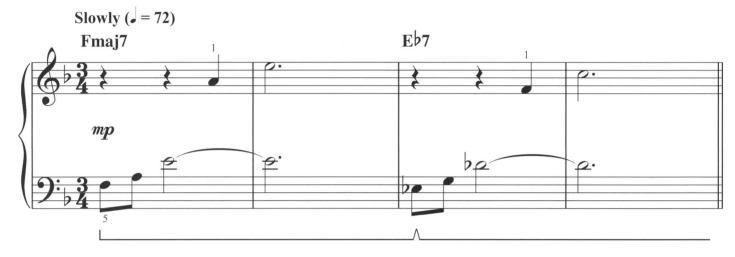

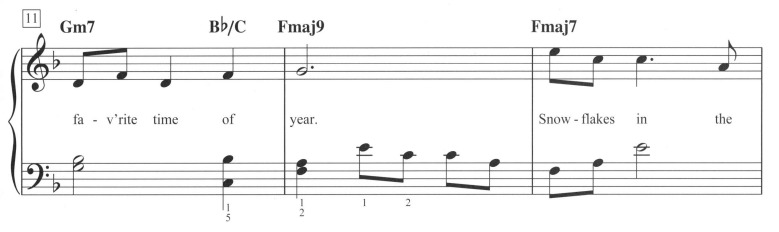

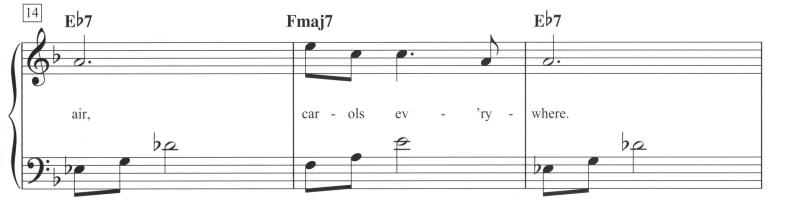

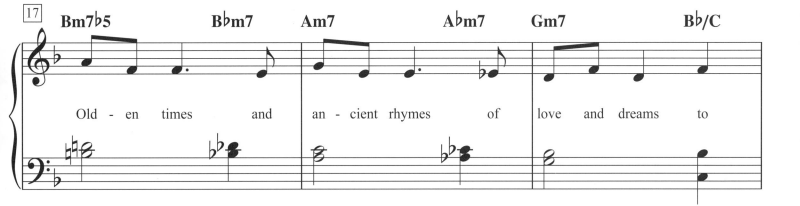

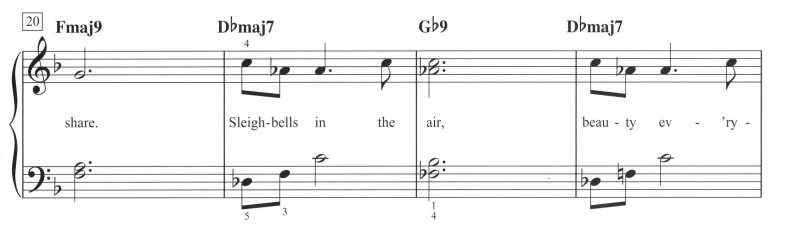

24

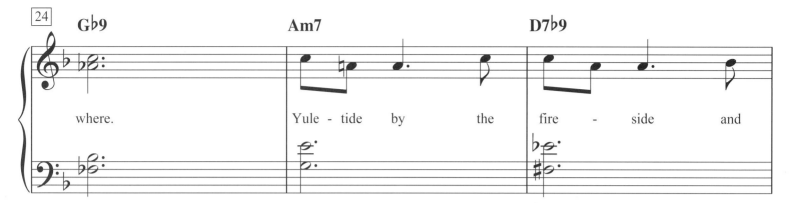

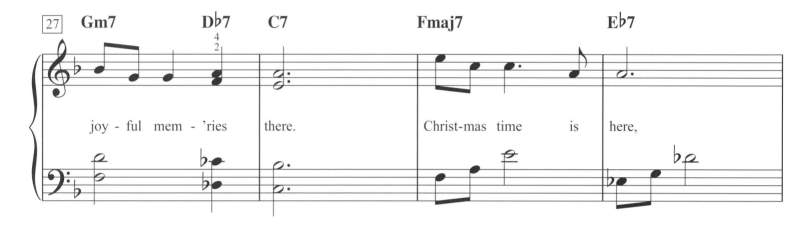

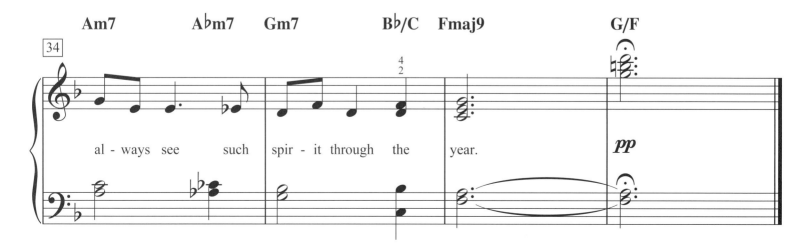

COUNT YOUR BLESSINGS INSTEAD OF SHEEP

from the Motion Picture Irving Berlin's WHITE CHRISTMAS

Words and Music by
IRVING BERLIN
Arranged by Phillip Keveren

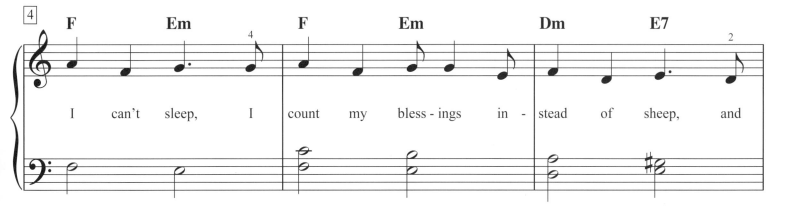

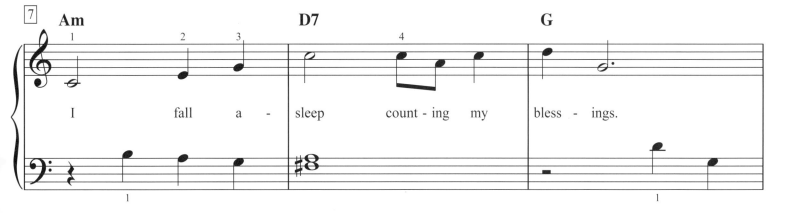

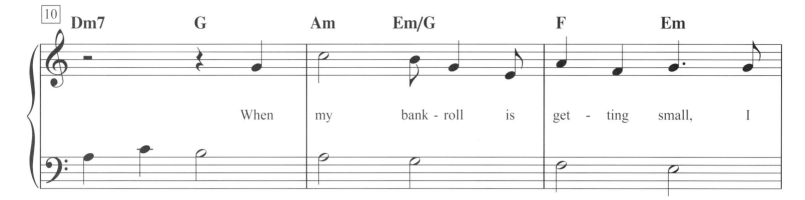

10 Dm7 | G | Am | Em/G | F | Em

When my bank - roll is get - ting small, I

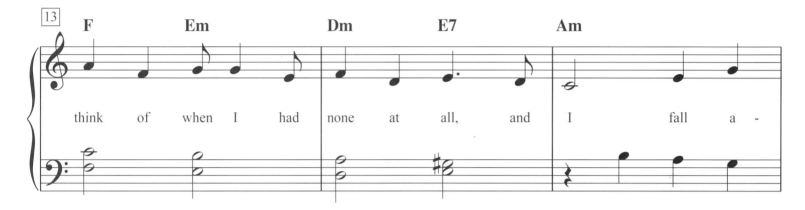

13 F | Em | Dm | E7 | Am

think of when I had none at all, and I fall a -

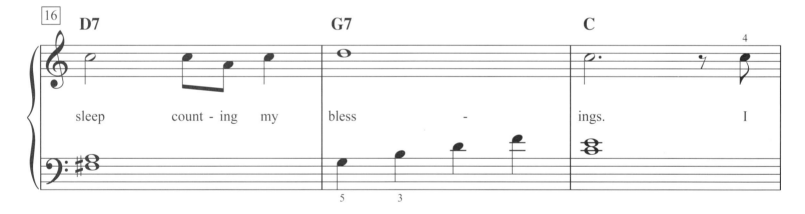

16 D7 | G7 | C

sleep count - ing my bless - ings. I

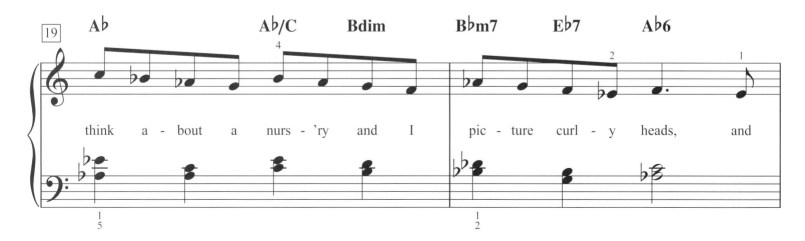

19 A♭ | A♭/C | Bdim | B♭m7 | E♭7 | A♭6

think a - bout a nurs - 'ry and I pic - ture curl - y heads, and

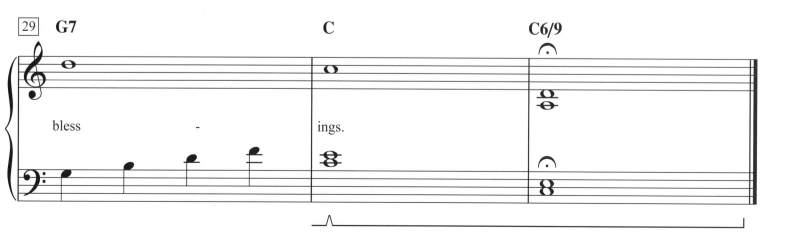

I WONDER AS I WANDER

By JOHN JACOB NILES
Arranged by Phillip Keveren

Expressively (♩ = 88)

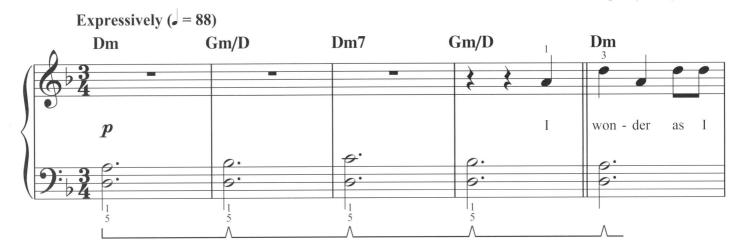

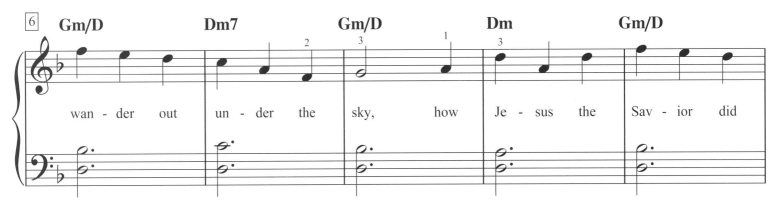

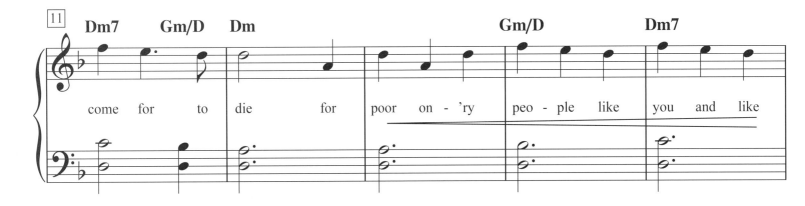

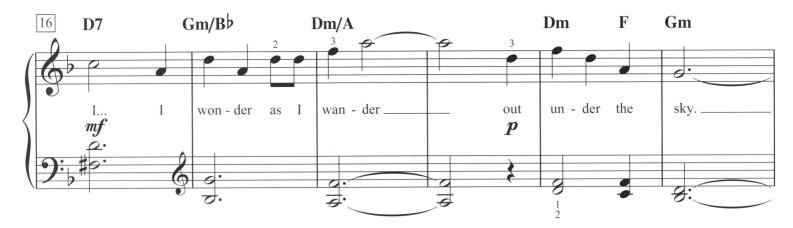

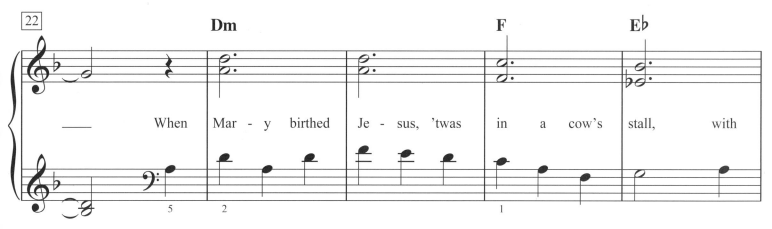

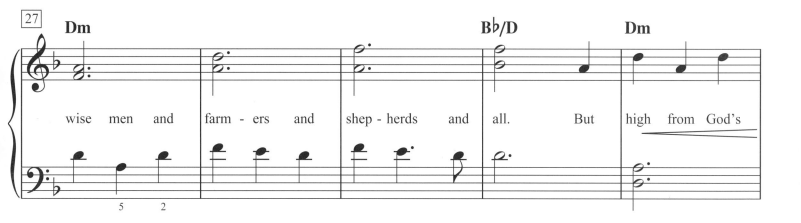

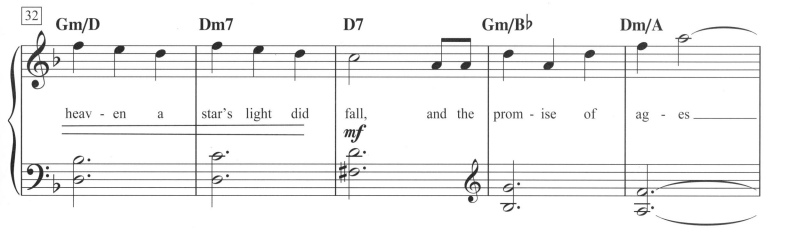

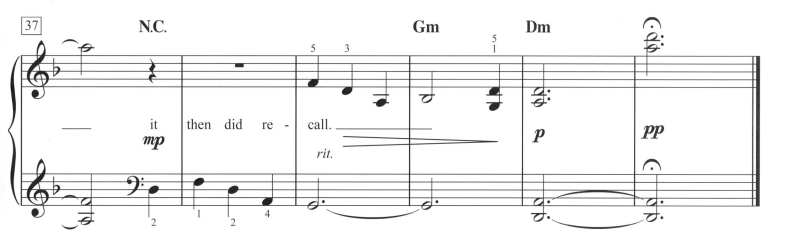

THE LITTLE DRUMMER BOY

Words and Music by HARRY SIMEONE,
HENRY ONORATI and KATHERINE DAVIS
Arranged by Phillip Keveren

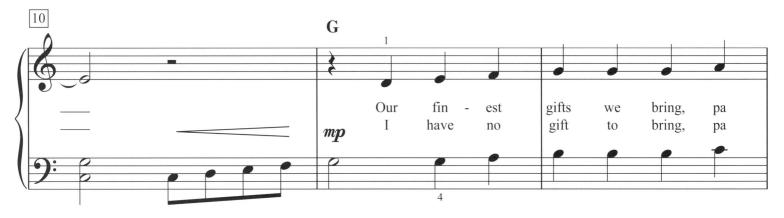

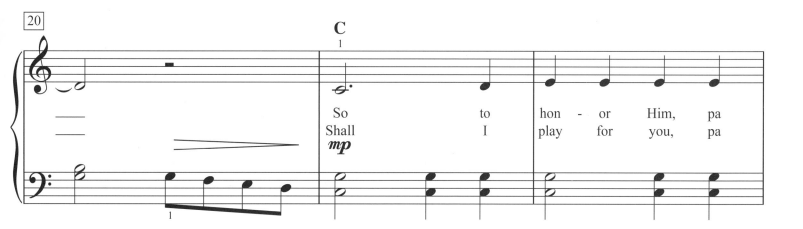

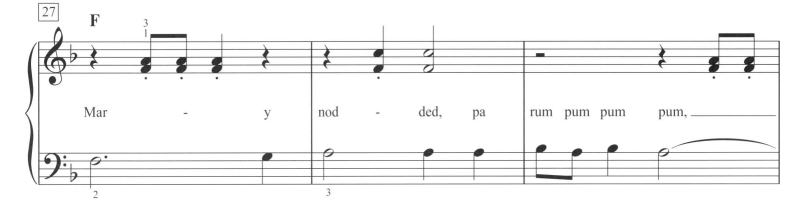

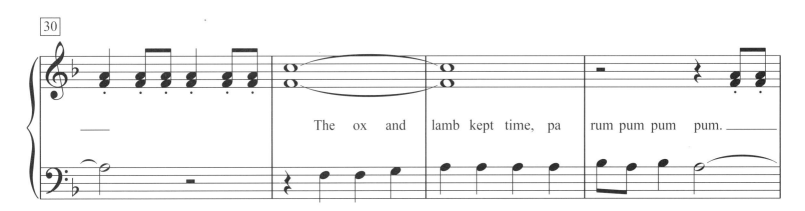

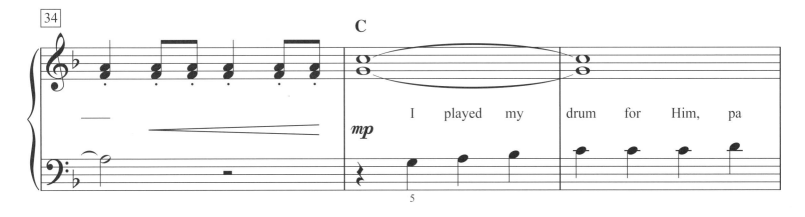

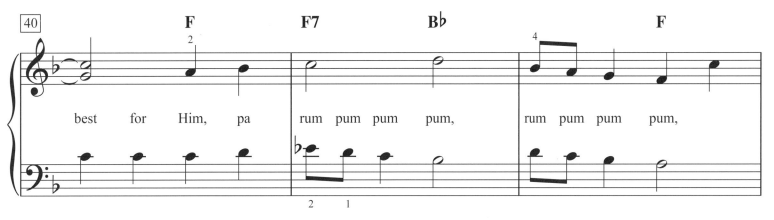

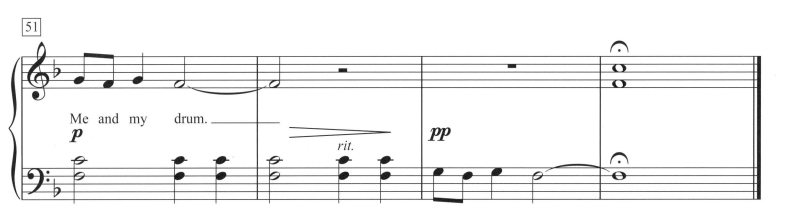

MARY, DID YOU KNOW?

Words and Music by MARK LOWRY
and BUDDY GREENE
Arranged by Phillip Keveren

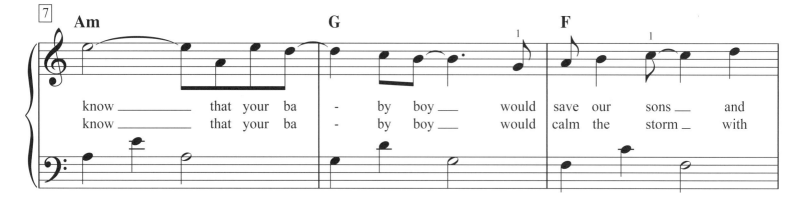

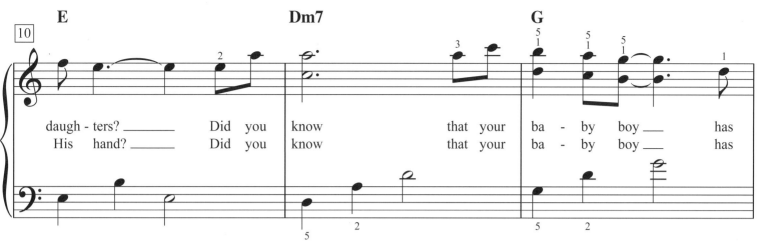

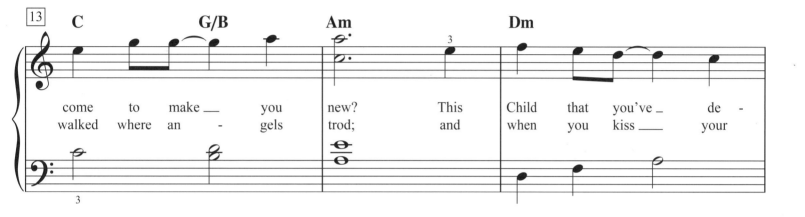

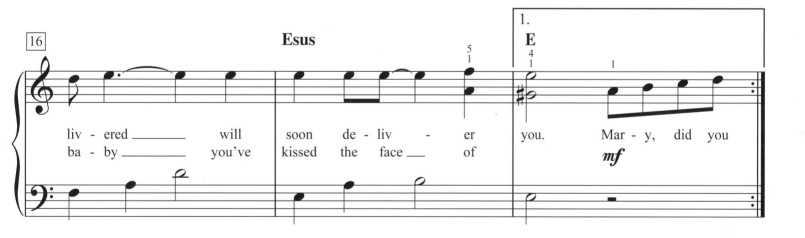

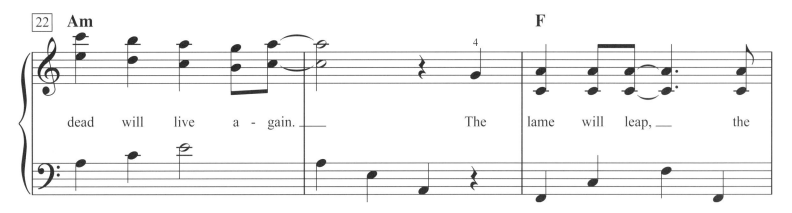

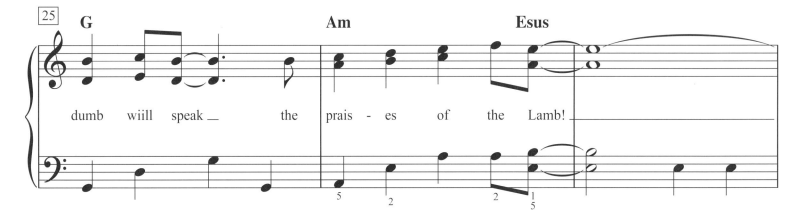

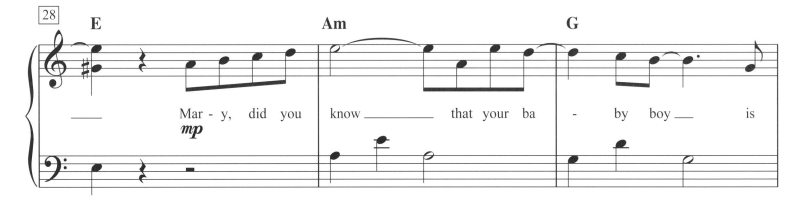

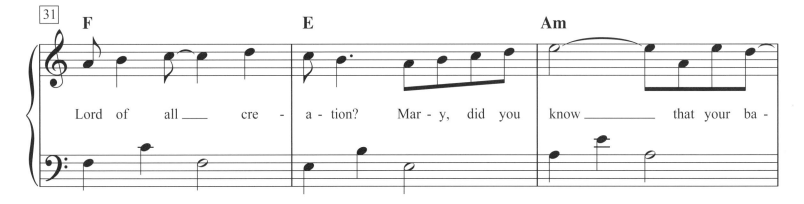

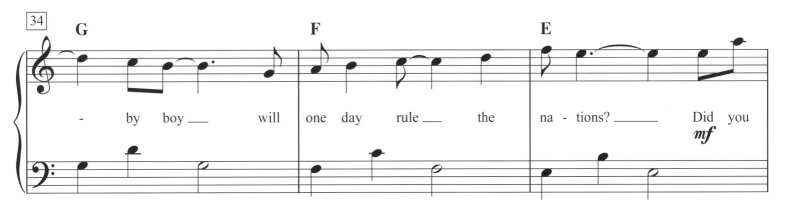

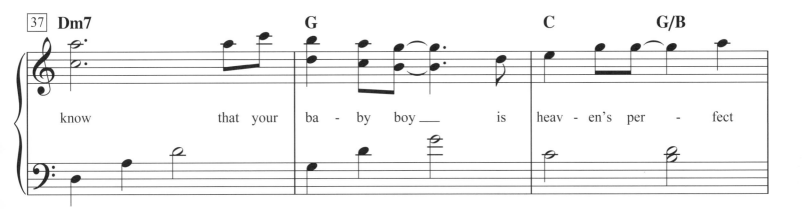

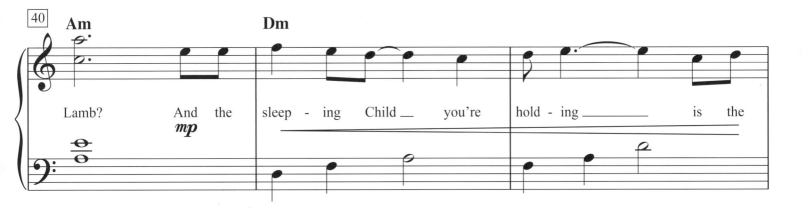

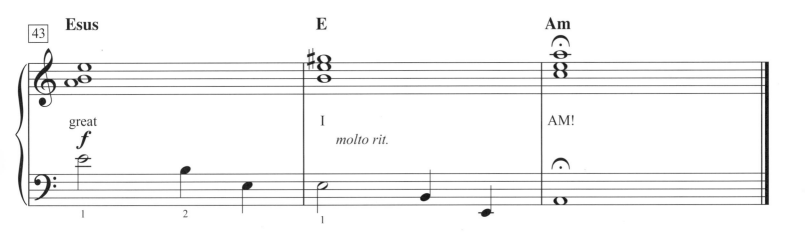

MERRY CHRISTMAS, DARLING

Words and Music by RICHARD CARPENTER
and FRANK POOLER
Arranged by Phillip Keveren

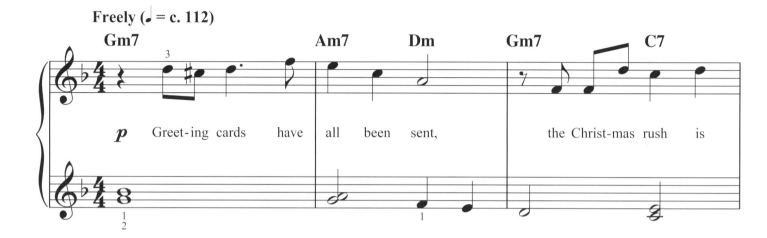

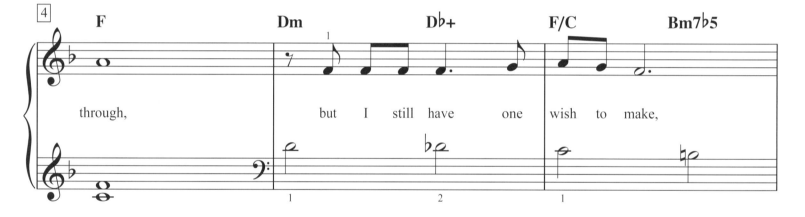

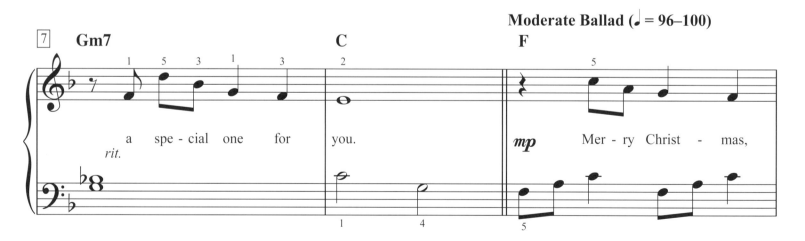

10 Gm/F　　　　　　　　F　　　　　　　　Cm7　　F7

dar - ling.　　　We're a - part,　that's true;　　but

13 B♭　　　C/B♭　　　Am7　　Dm/A　　Gm7　　Am

I　can dream　and　in　my dreams,　I'm　Christ - mas - ing　with

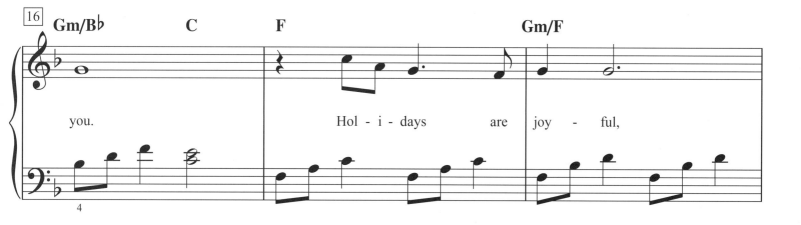

16 Gm/B♭　　　C　　F　　　　　　　Gm/F

you.　　　Hol - i - days　are　joy - ful,

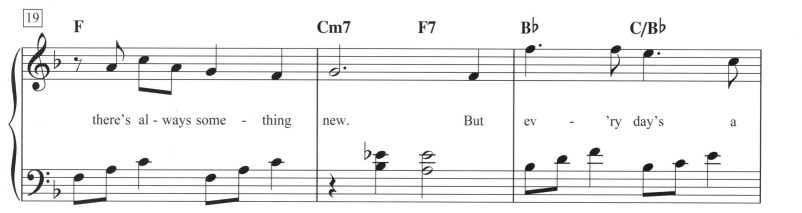

19 F　　　　　　　　Cm7　　F7　　B♭　　C/B♭

there's al - ways some - thing　new.　　But　ev - 'ry day's　a

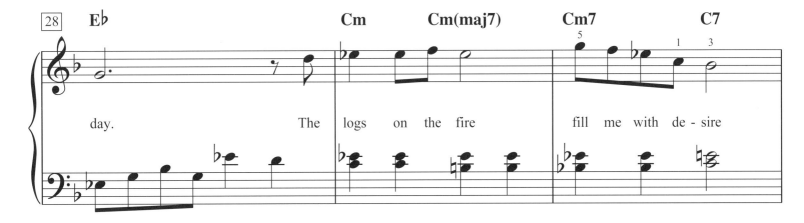

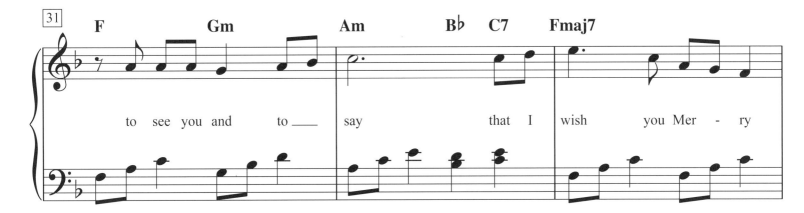

Christ - mas, Hap - py New Year, too. I've

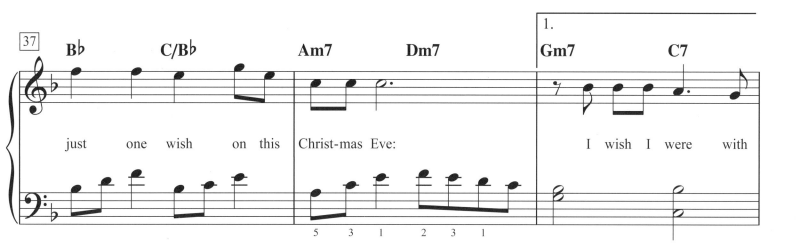

just one wish on this Christ-mas Eve: I wish I were with

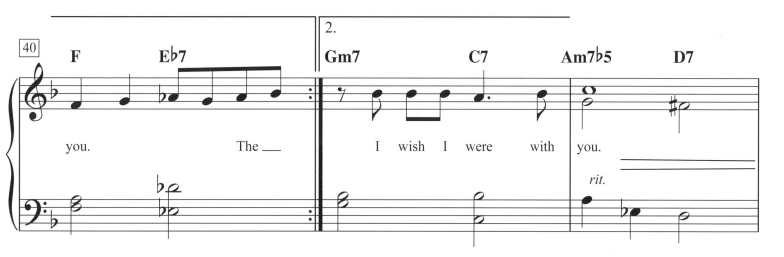

you. The ___ I wish I were with you. *rit.*

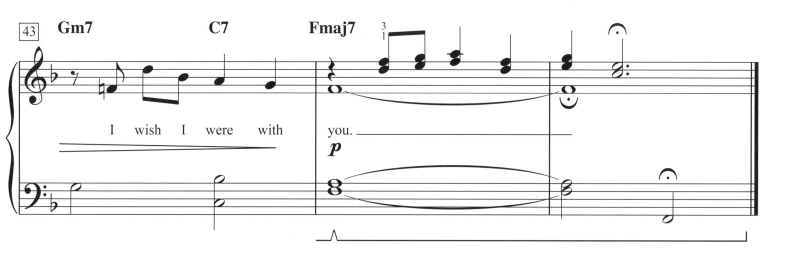

I wish I were with you. *p*

RIVER

Words and Music by
JONI MITCHELL
Arranged by Phillip Keveren

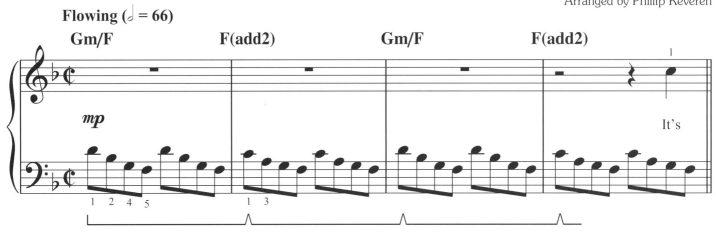

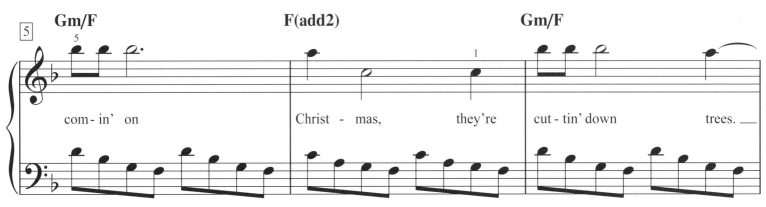

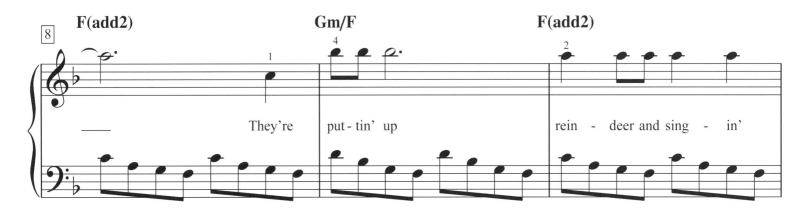

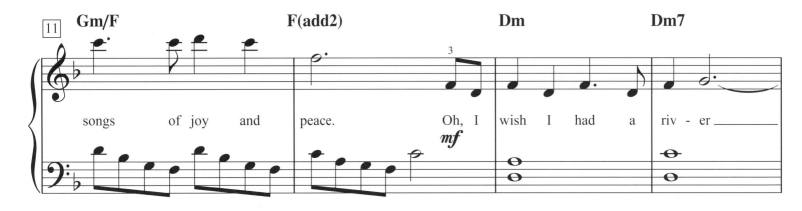

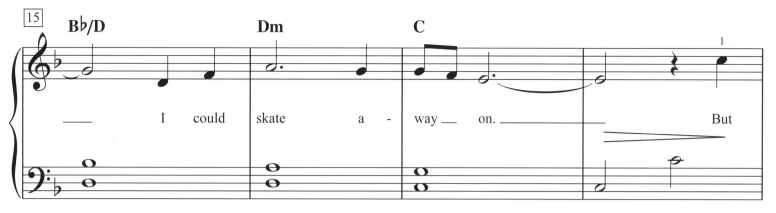

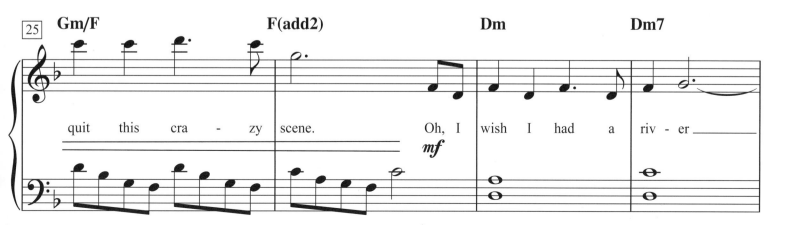

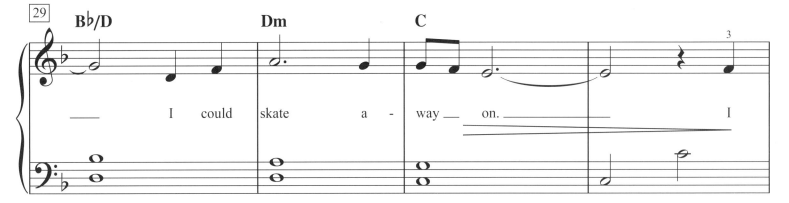

I could skate a - way __ on. __ I

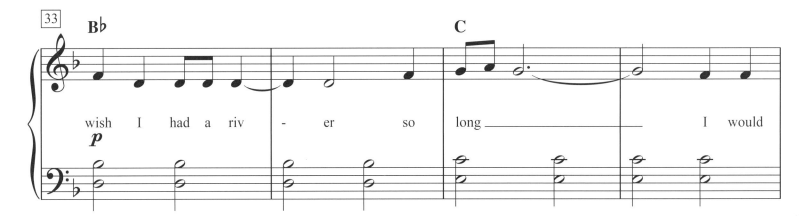

wish I had a riv - er so long __ I would

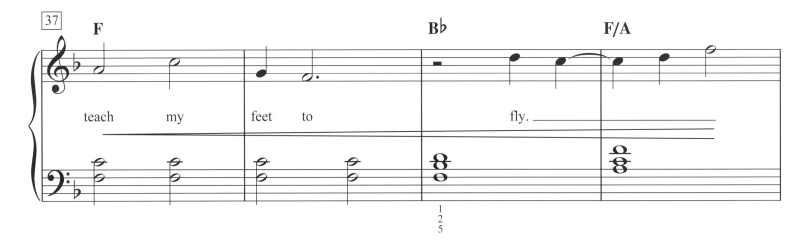

teach my feet to fly. __

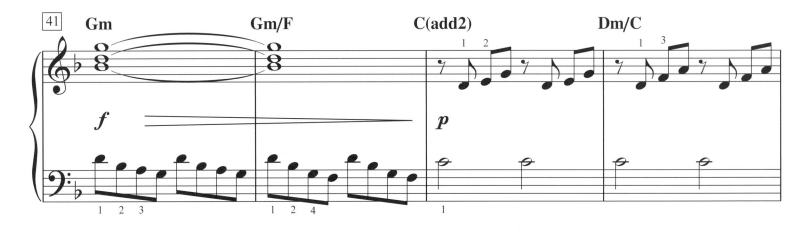

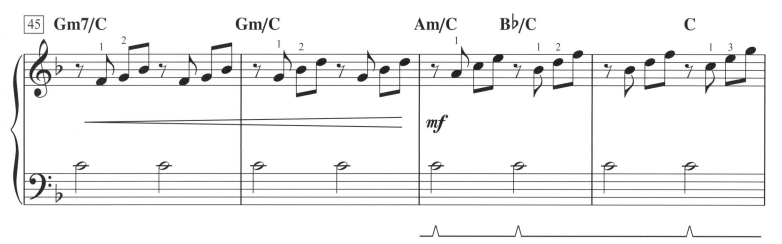

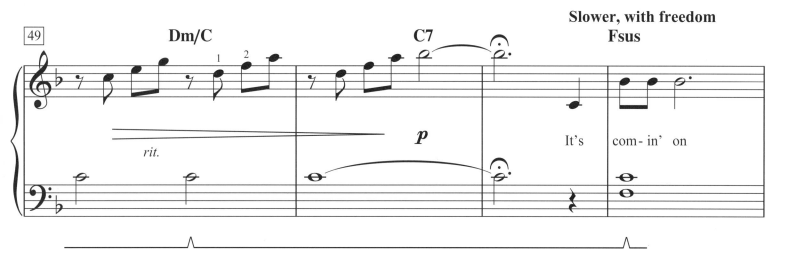

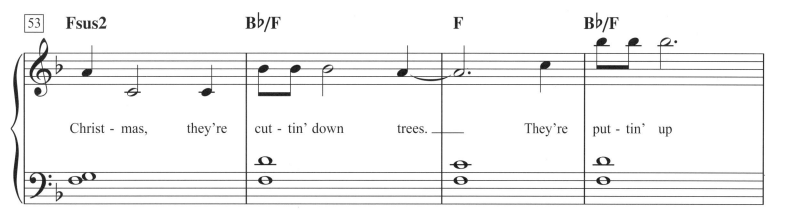

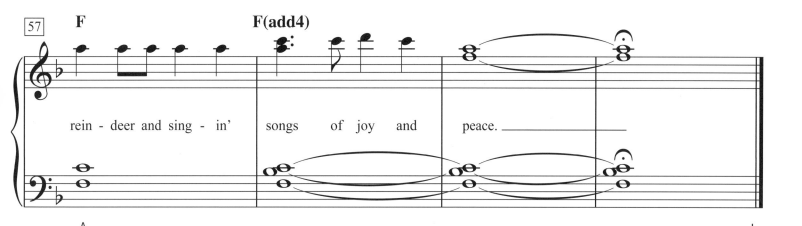

SILVER AND GOLD

Music and Lyrics by
JOHNNY MARKS
Arranged by Phillip Keveren

Delicate Waltz (♩ = 126)

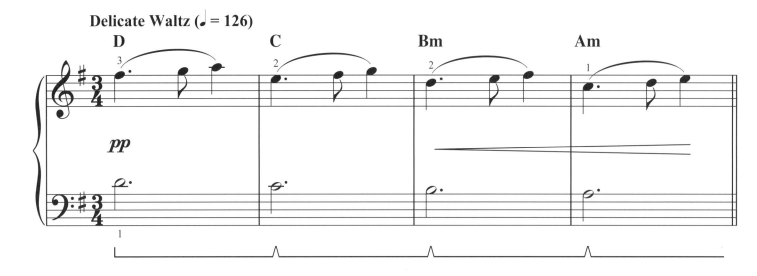

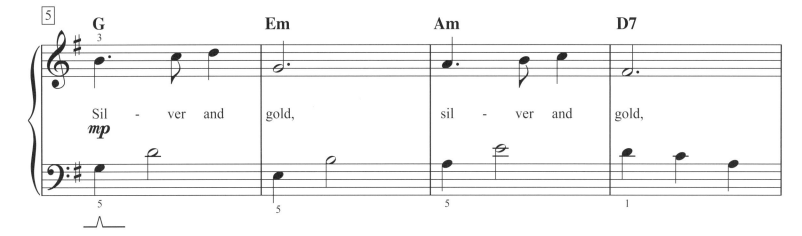

Sil - ver and gold, sil - ver and gold,

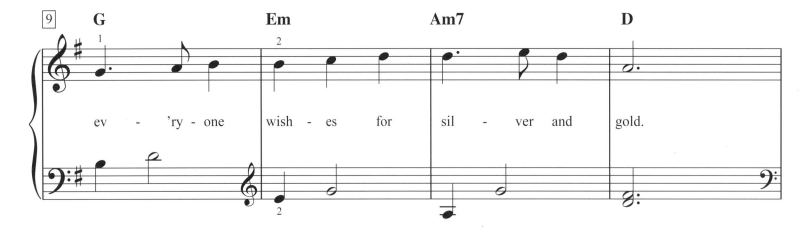

ev - 'ry - one wish - es for sil - ver and gold.

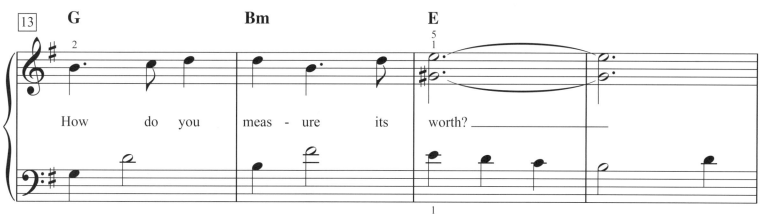

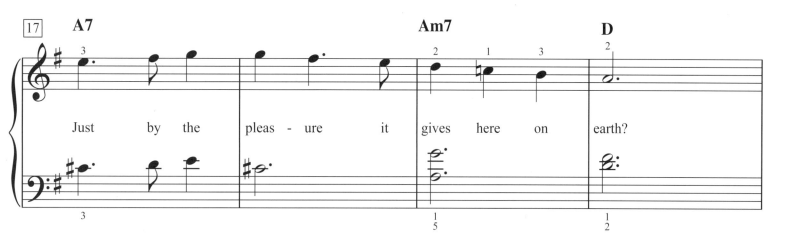

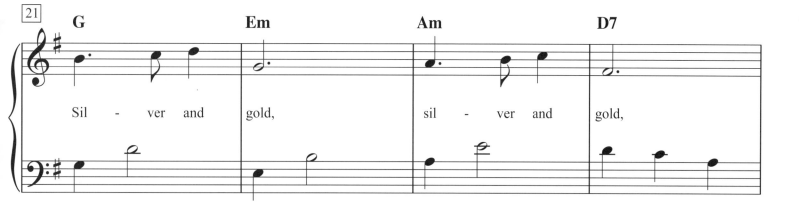

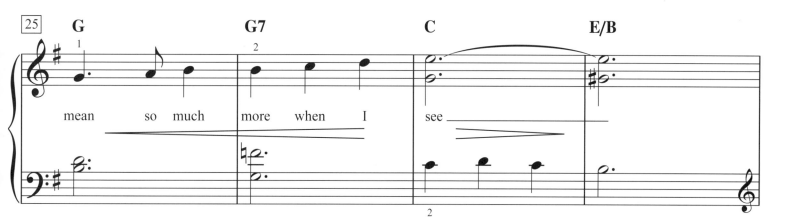

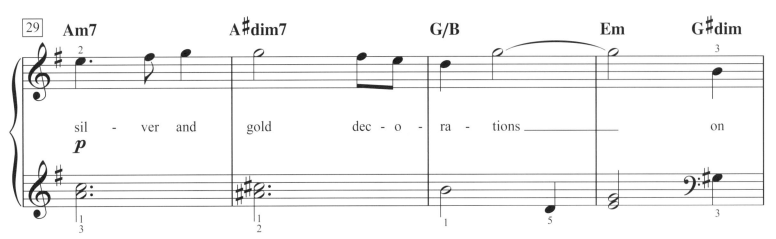

sil - ver and gold dec - o - ra - tions _____ on

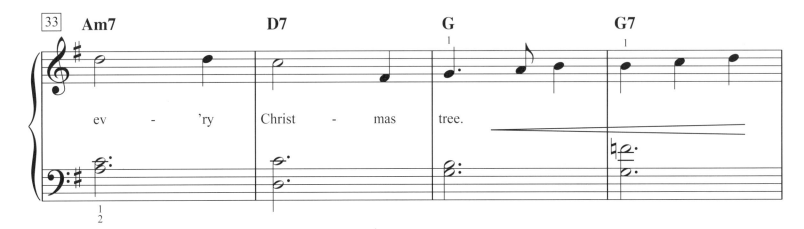

ev - 'ry Christ - mas tree.

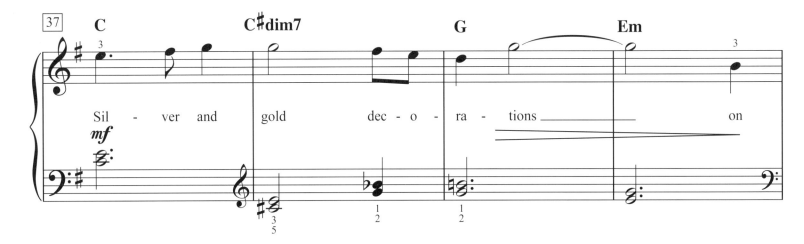

Sil - ver and gold dec - o - ra - tions _____ on

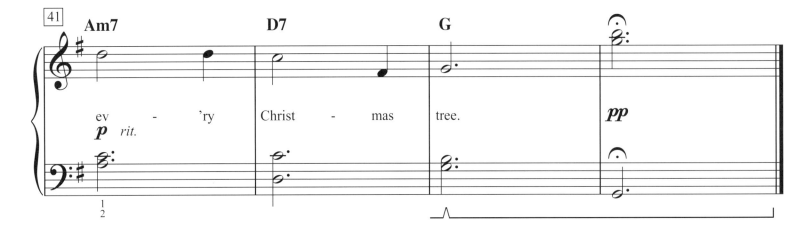

ev - 'ry Christ - mas tree.

WHITE CHRISTMAS

from the Motion Picture Irving Berlin's HOLIDAY INN

Words and Music by
IRVING BERLIN
Arranged by Phillip Keveren

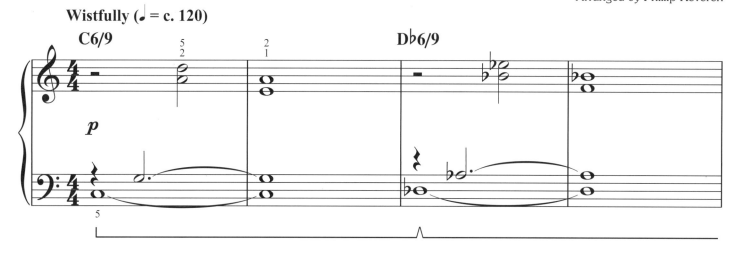

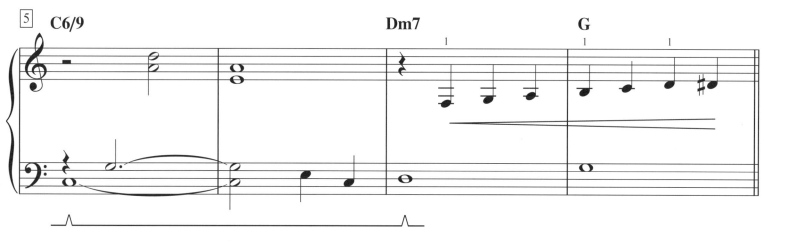

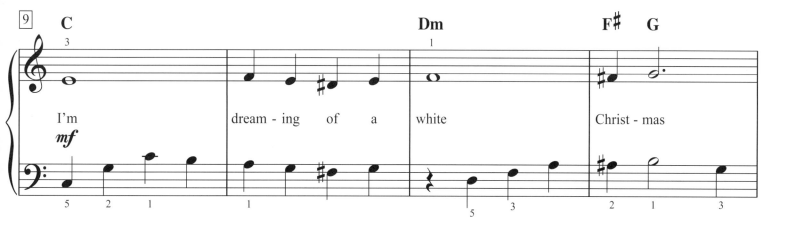

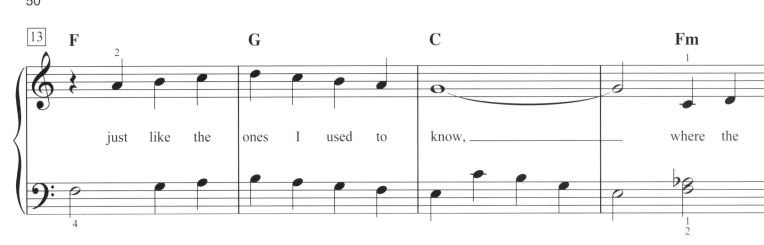

just like the ones I used to know, _____ where the

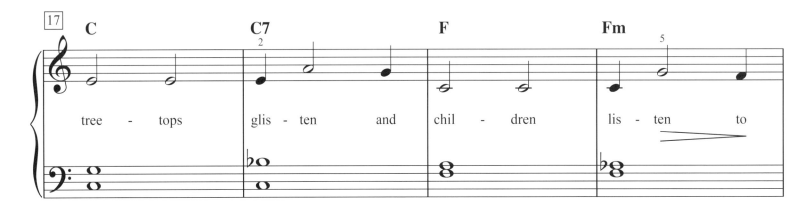

tree - tops glis - ten and chil - dren lis - ten to

hear sleigh - bells in the snow. _____

I'm dream - ing of a white

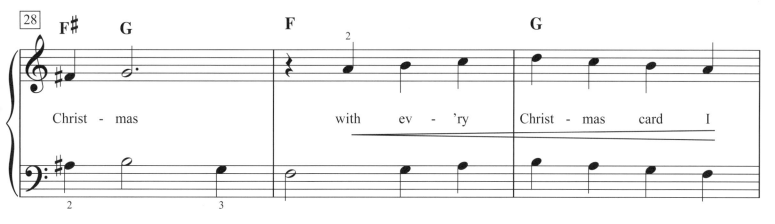

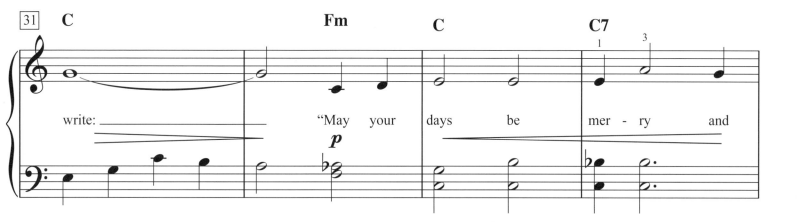

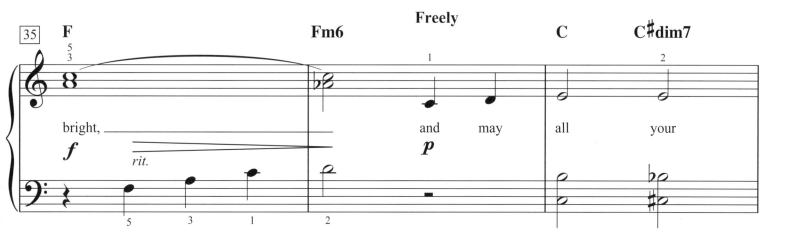

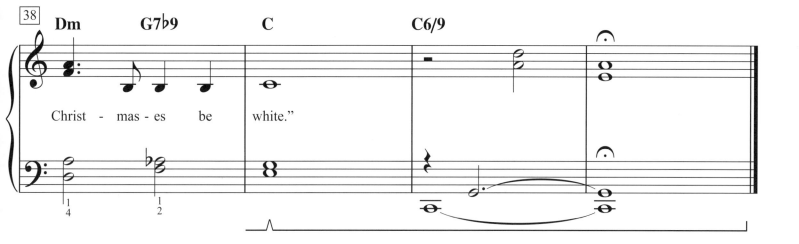

STAR OF BETHLEHEM
from the Twentieth Century Fox Motion Picture HOME ALONE

Words by LESLIE BRICUSSE
Music by JOHN WILLIAMS
Arranged by Phillip Keveren

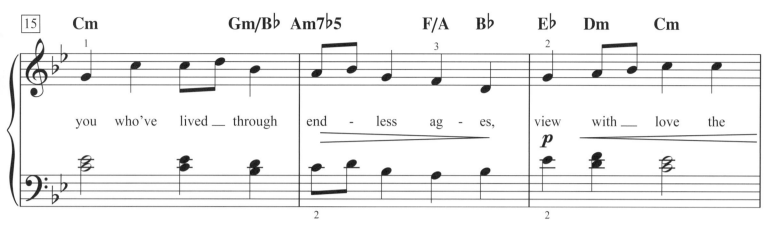

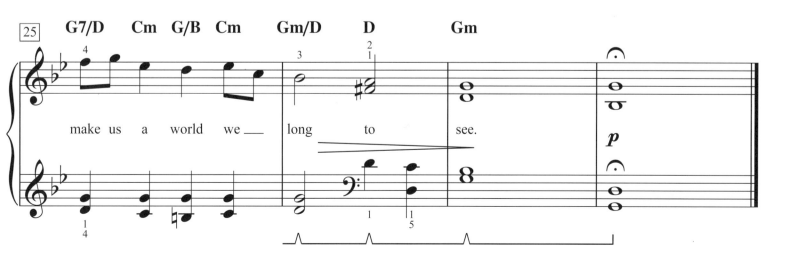

WELCOME TO OUR WORLD

Words and Music by
CHRIS RICE
Arranged by Phillip Keveren

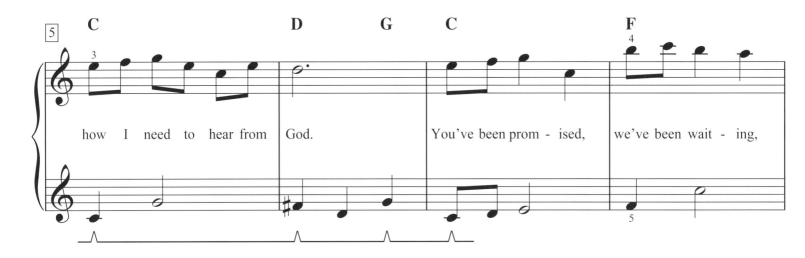

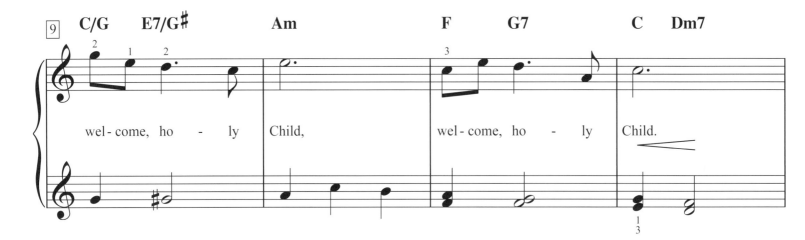

Hope that You don't mind our man - ger, how I wish we would have

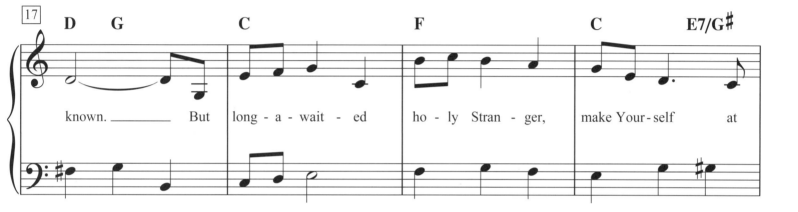

known. _____ But long - a - wait - ed ho - ly Stran - ger, make Your - self at

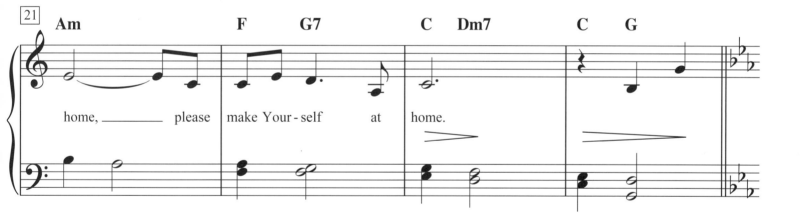

home, _____ please make Your - self at home.

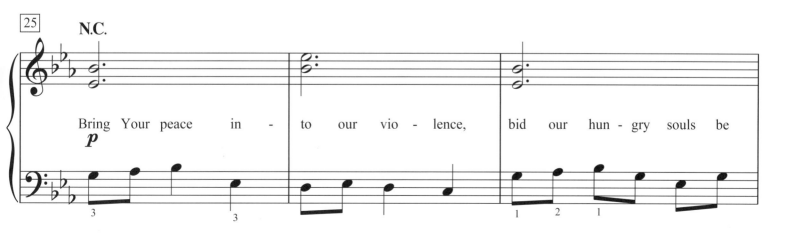

Bring Your peace in - to our vio - lence, bid our hun - gry souls be

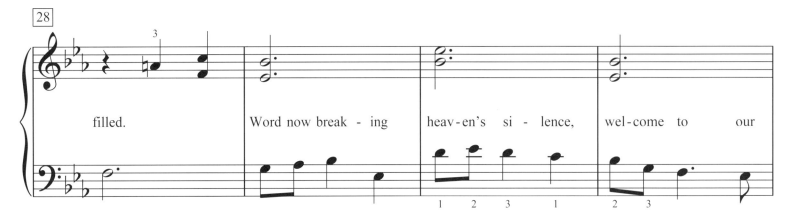

filled. Word now break - ing heav-en's si - lence, wel-come to our

world, wel-come to our world. Frag - ile fin - ger

mp

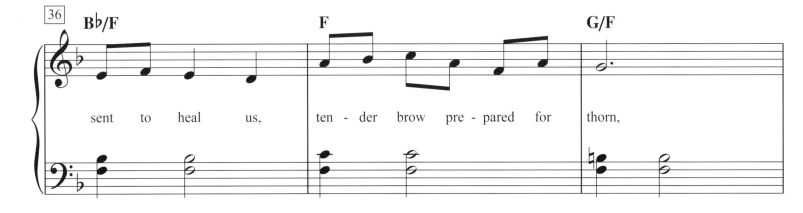

sent to heal us, ten - der brow pre - pared for thorn,

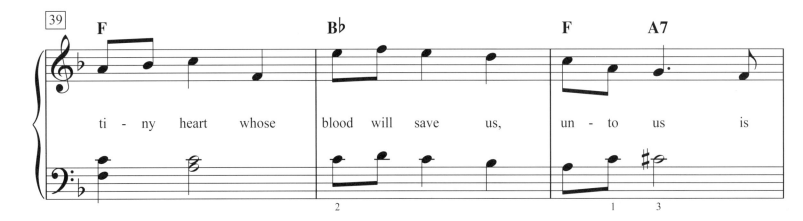

ti - ny heart whose blood will save us, un - to us is

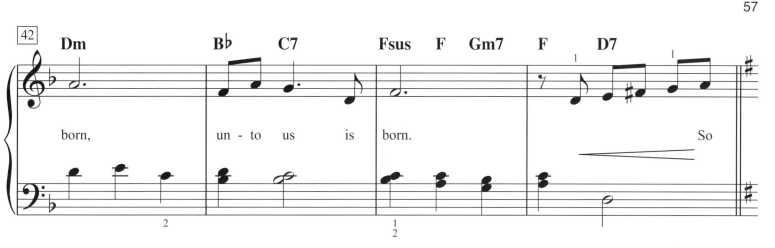

born, un-to us is born. So

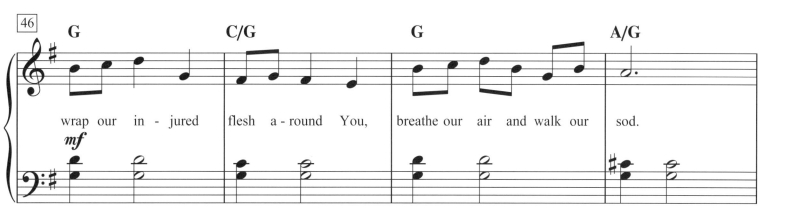

wrap our in-jured flesh a-round You, breathe our air and walk our sod.

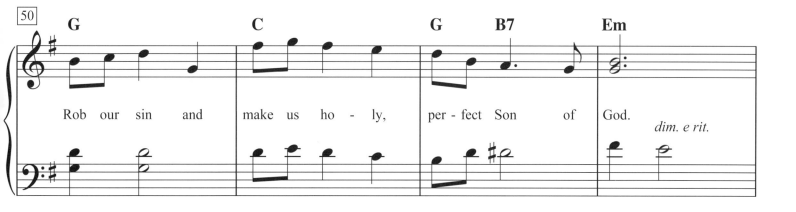

Rob our sin and make us ho - ly, per-fect Son of God.

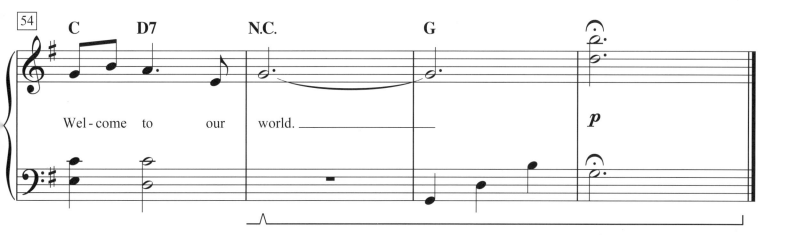

Wel-come to our world. _____

WHO WOULD IMAGINE A KING

from THE PREACHER'S WIFE

Words and Music by MERVYN WARREN
and HALLERIN HILTON HILL
Arranged by Phillip Keveren

Gently (♩ = 96)

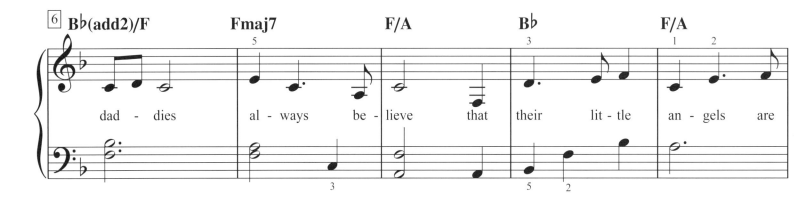

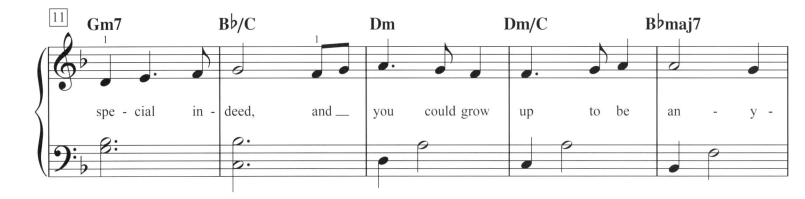

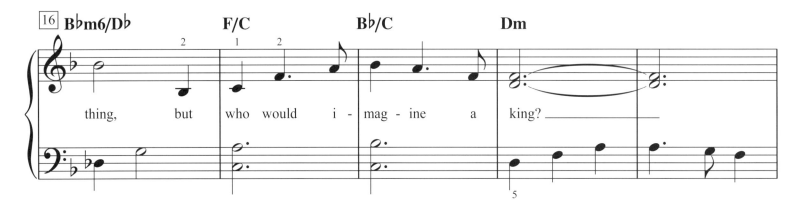

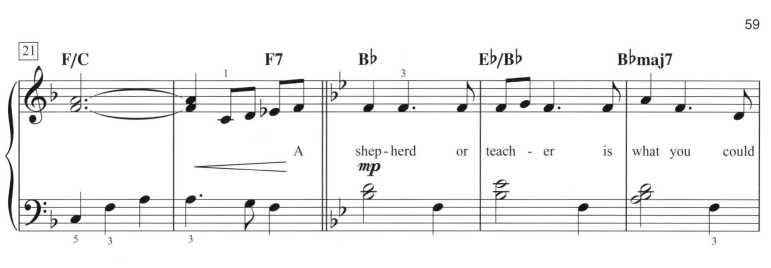

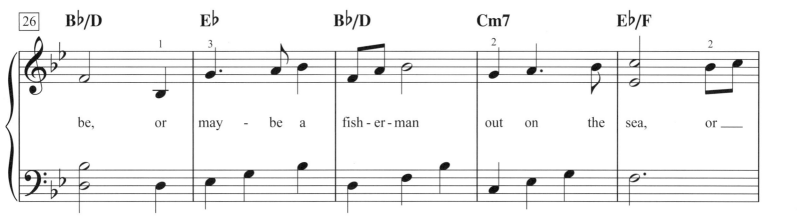

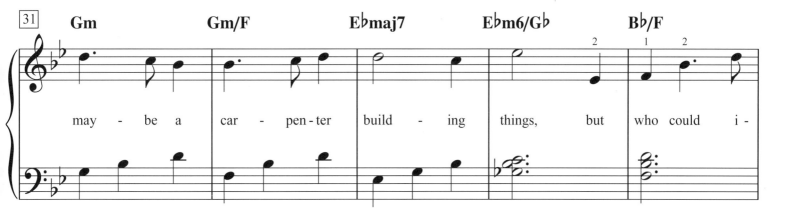

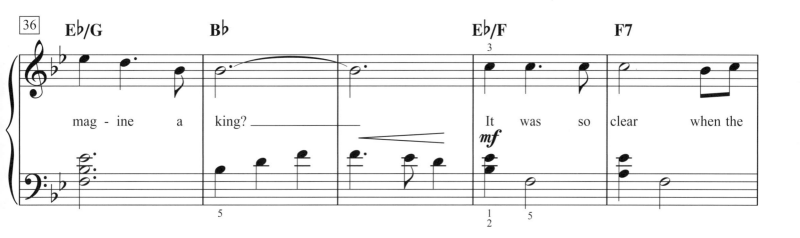

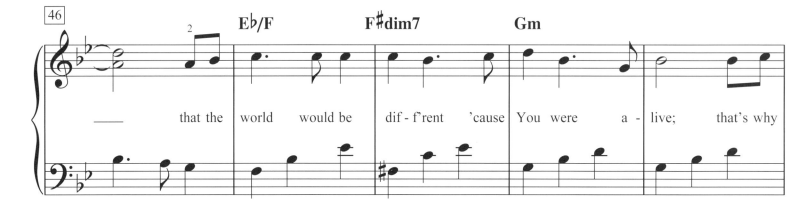

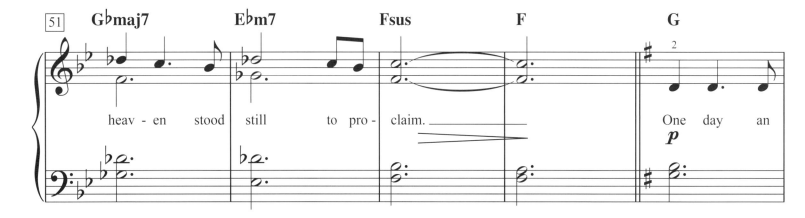

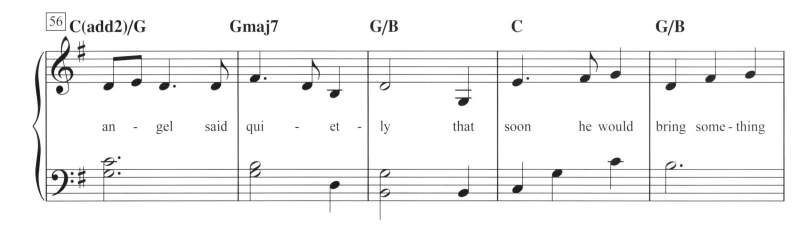

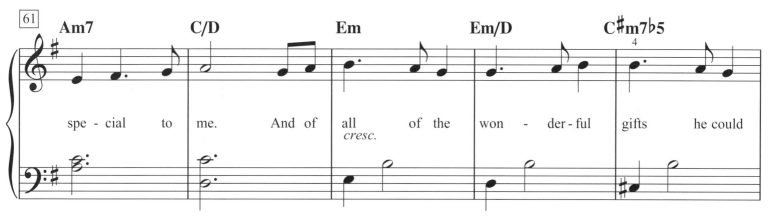

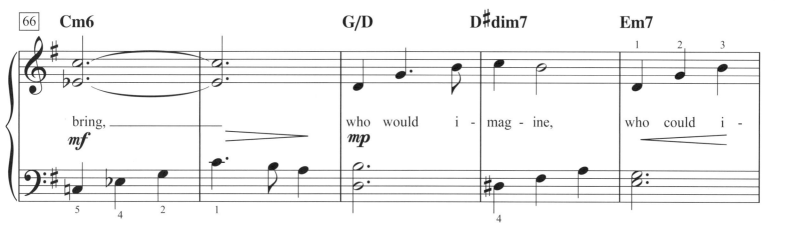

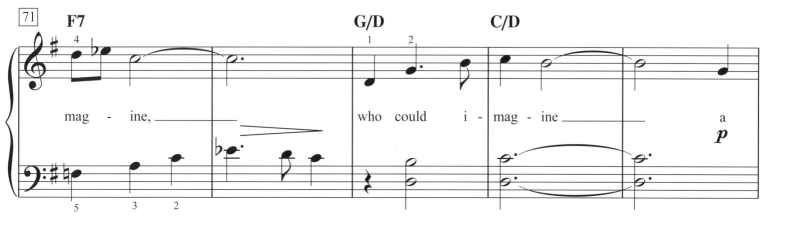

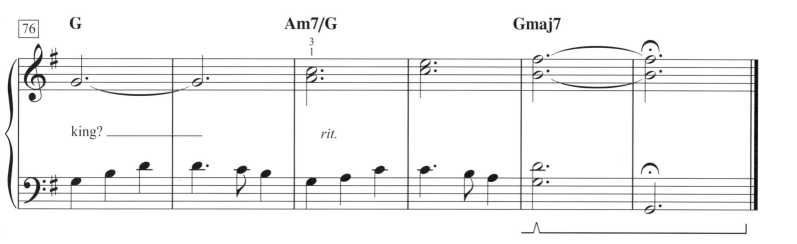

WHAT ARE YOU DOING NEW YEAR'S EVE?

By FRANK LOESSER
Arranged by Phillip Keveren

Sentimentally (♩. = 72)

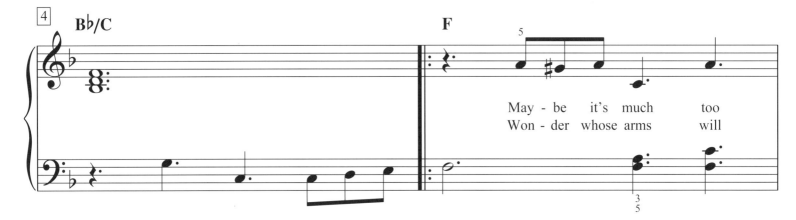

May - be it's much too
Won - der whose arms will

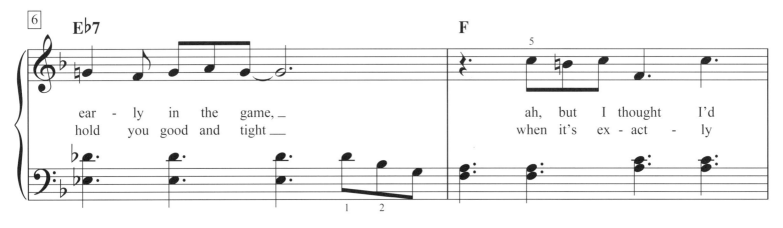

ear - ly in the game, __ ah, but I thought I'd
hold you good and tight __ when it's ex - act - ly

ask you just the same, __ what are you do - ing the new year's,
twelve o'-clock at night, __ wel - com - ing in the new year,

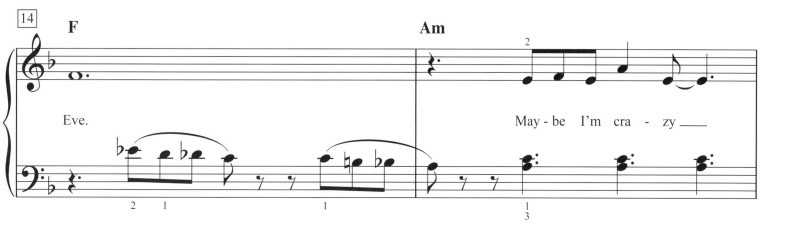

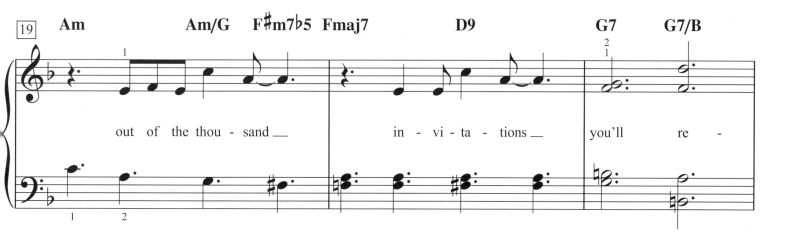

ceive.

Ah, but in case I

stand one lit - tle chance, _

here comes the jack - pot

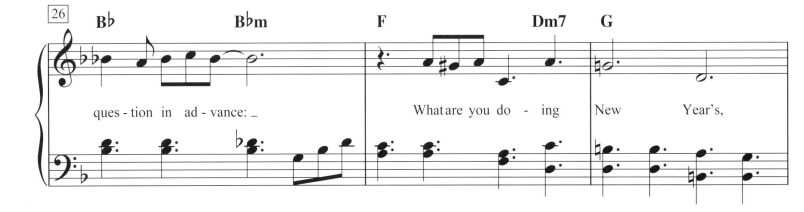

ques - tion in ad - vance: _

What are you do - ing New Year's,

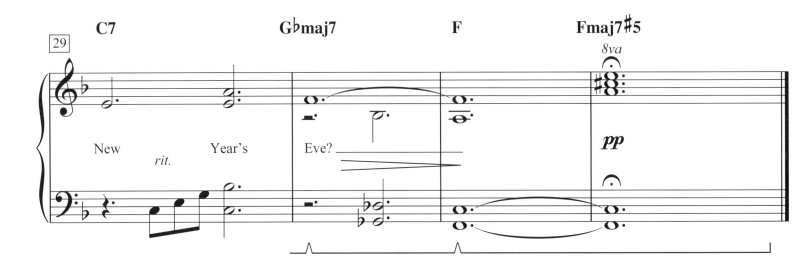

New Year's Eve?